Jim G.

Letters to the Grandchildren
1995-2015

Cover and illustrations by Mary Younker
Letters compiled by Lori Younker

December 2015

*Dedicated to
the grandchildren of James and Wanda Gerdeen*

*Peter, Joanna, Harlan
Mary, Skye, Connor*

INTRODUCTION

James C. Gerdeen is known simply by his friends as "Jim." Communicating regularly with his grandchildren was a commitment he made in the 1990s. Most of this communication was made via electronic mail (email) since its inception. It has been my joy and privilege to gather his letters and to place them "under one roof."

As we were growing up, my father lived out the faith of Jesus in realness, genuine caring, patience, and gentleness with Sonya, Tim and me. It wasn't hard to imagine a loving God in heaven because our dad did such a good job at reflecting Jesus Christ. I always felt safe just knowing my father was somewhere on the planet, always ready to receive my phone call.

Here in these letters, he reminds all of us of the right way to live. If our family would heed his encouragement to follow after right living, we will truly be blessed. If you've already strayed or are on your way back to the arms of Jesus, these letters will remind you of the complete acceptance we have in our Savior. It is possible to finish out well, living not for self, but for God.

When I was a teen, Dad was incredibly busy. My siblings and I might have longed for more time with him. He was a successful professor, a man of research, an advisor and even a pastor of two churches at one time. However, when my children were young, he went to the Promise Keepers Conference where he renewed his desire to spend time with his grandchildren.

It must have been so tough to see my family whisked off to the other side of the world—right when he was so willing to dedicate himself to their growth. Yet, he committed himself to write. Since he and Mom lived in Colorado at that time, he named his newsletters, "*Caws from Crow Hill*, and later, *Echoes from Colorado*. When I read his letters, I picture him on the top of a mountain cliff, like a majestic wolf, howling out into the night, imploring us to follow the true way of wisdom.

Thank you, Dad. Thank you, Grandpa. Thank you, Jim for being who you are and sharing yourself with us.   –Lori Younker, *October, 2015*

CAWS FROM CROW HILL
August 10, 1995

Caw! Caw! Caw!

Sounds heard at 5:30 a.m. through the bedroom window at 221 Delwood Drive.

Crows are still cawing.

Six or more hummingbirds are still humming.

Dozen or more birds are still feeding.

Chipmunks still running

Ebony still chasing.

Peter's tree house is still in the tree.

God is still on the throne.

Jesus is still Savior.

Holy Spirit is still the Comforter.

CAWS (CAUSE) FROM CROW HILL
Bailey, Colorado
October 10, 1995

This month I want to write to you about the "cause" from Crow Hill. "Cause" not caws, 'cause I have not seen any crows lately. Peter, his Dad, and I saw a lot of crows while fishing in Mongolia. Peter caught a big 20 inch trout. His Dad and I caught nothing. "Cause" not "bee-caws" or (because), "cause there are not any bees on Crow Hill either. Too cold now. Not many bees in summer, either.

We all need a cause to live for. Cause is like a purpose. Not porpoise, 'cause there are not any porpoises in Colorado either, 'cause there are not any oceans here. We all need a cause to live for. Peter, Joanna, Mary, Lori, and Bill are in Mongolia 'cause God called them there.

We need to do our very best in school 'cause our creator God gave us abilities, and He is pleased when we fulfill His plan for us. We need to be kind and friendly because we want to be a good witness. But it is hard to be good without God's help, 'cause we are born in sin into a sinful world.

So we have a 'cause to pray, read God's Word and thank Him for his help, 'cause it is the best way to live. I write to you 'cause I love you, and 'cause I want you to find God's best for your life. That's the "cause" from Crow Hill this month. Excuse Grandpa's play on words. By the way, don't spell the word *because* as "bee-caws" or you will flunk Spelling. *Love, Your Colorado Grandpa*

CALLS (CAWS) FROM CROW HILL
November 10, 1995

```
_____
<||||>>< caw, caw, caw
 / \
```

Caws from crows are not the only calls from Crow Hill. Yes, there are caws when crows send a warning when they see a stranger like me or Ebony, our dog. But sometimes we hear squirrels calling. They sort of chatter. Then one night, Wanda and I awoke, it sounded like the elk calling, sort of a strange squeaky sound. Of course there is the fire siren calling, and we see firemen come driving fast to the station to catch a fire truck or ambulance to answer an emergency call. When Ebony hears the siren, she begins a mournful howl in answer, like a call of the wild.

Ebony and I heard a strange bird call today as we walked up the mountain. We did not recognize it. If we belonged to that bird's family, we probably would have understood. It reminded me of God's call. Many do not hear, because they are too busy and noisy to hear. Others hear the call, but they do not recognize it, because they are not of God's family and do not speak God's language.

God's language in the Bible has been translated to simple English so we can hear. When we ask God to help get the ungodly dirt out of our ears, we hear God calling. What do we hear?

God calling, *"Come follow Me," "Come unto Me,"*

"Honor thy Father and Mother, that thy days may be long on the land which God gives to you," and **"For God so loved** (us), *that He gave His only Son* (Jesus), *that whosoever* (put your name here) *believes in Him* (Jesus), *may have eternal life* (live forever with God).

God's calls are sometimes warnings too, like crows cawing. "Thou shall not steal" and "Thou shall not lie." Because if we do, we get into trouble.

There is a call that in November, we should especially hear and obey. Can you fill in the "blanks: *"In everything give _____for this is God's _____in _____ _____ concerning you."*

Hint: You can find the verse in the N.T. in one of Paul's letters.

Calls. God's calls. Do you hear them?

Love, and warm fuzzy feelings, Your Colorado Grandpa

P.S. (Grandpa) tried to draw a crow with the keyboard. Can you do better? If so, send me your crow.

"CULLS" FROM CROW HILL
December 16, 1995

Instead of caws or calls, I think of culls this Christmas. Do you know what a "cull" is? When Grandpa was a boy he worked in the woods with his dad and his grandpa and uncles in the forests of Upper Michigan. We would cut cedar posts and peel them, but we "culled" out the crooked ones and the much too skinny ones. They were "culls" or rejects.

When we as a family lived in Minneapolis, we would go to a tree lot to pick out a Christmas tree. Of course we looked for the best. After Christmas there were still some scrawny trees left. They were the culls that nobody wanted. Also, on our property on Crow Hill there are some crooked trees with uneven branches. We do not have to worry about someone stealing one, because they are culls.

Culls remind me of Christmas and the baby Jesus. Why? Because He was a cull. Did you know this? The Bible says He was not very pretty and no one desired Him. The Bible says He was like a stone that the builders rejected. But really He came from Heaven where He was God and where He is beautiful and glorious.

To understand this, I would like you to draw and color two Christmas trees. Make one big and beautiful to represent Jesus as God in heaven. Make one small and ugly, like the baby Jesus He became. Why did Jesus become like this little cull? He did it to become like one of us, so we would know that He loves us. You see sometimes people reject us or they call us names like ugly or something. But the good news of Christmas is that baby Jesus came to be our friend.

There is more to it than that. He also became like us, a cull, so we could become like Him in heaven. The Bible says if we are a friend of Baby Jesus, that someday He will make us beautiful and glorious like He is in Heaven. What a friend! Thank you, Jesus!

Do you understand? If not, ask your Mom and Dad. Maybe they can answer your question.

At this point Sonya has not had her Baby yet. We will leave for KC as soon as she does.

CAWS FROM CROW HILL
January 13, 1996

Dear Mary, Joanna, and Peter:

My December letter was sent as an attachment to an email, so maybe you did not get it, according to your dad. So I am sending a copy of the December letter with this one.

The reason I write Grandpa newsletters is because I miss being able to visit with you. So I write letters instead. I remember good times I had with my grandpas and grandmas.

My Grandmother, Anna Gerdeen, died when I was only 2 years old in 1939. She had diabetes. I don't remember much about her. My Great Grandpa Gustav Johnson died when I was only 4 years old in 1941. He was 94. I remember he always had pink peppermint candy for me, when we would visit him in Bark River, MI.

My Grandpa Theodore Gerdeen (Gustav's son) died when I was only 14 years old in 1951. He was 74 and was found dead in the woods from a heart attack. I remember the many times he was over to our house for Sunday dinner. I enjoyed listening to him tell us about the prophecies of the end of the world when Jesus was coming back again. He was a devout Christian.

My Grandpa Carl Jule Johnson died in 1963. He was about 68 years old. He lived next door to us in the country. In fact, he gave my

Dad land to build a house when I was born. Grandpa Johnson taught me to hunt rabbits and deer. We hunted many times together. He had an excellent rabbit dog named Danny, a bluetick hound that could find rabbits when no other dog could. I loved to listen to Grandpa's hunting stories—especially in the old days in lumber camps when he could shoot all the deer he wanted for the hunting camp. One day in the Depression days when everyone was so poor they were running out of pancake flour, the camp cook mixed sawdust with the flour. It was so bad, Grandpa said, that the dogs wouldn't even eat the pancakes. After tasting them, they licked their butts to get the taste out of their mouths.

My Grandma Anna Johnson died in 1968. She was such a devout Christian and may be the reason many of us are Christians today. She prayed so much for her children, grandchildren, and great grandchildren. She often spent sleepless nights crying and praying for us. Her mother died when she was only 8 years old I think. But Grandma accepted Jesus when she was a little girl, and she lived for Jesus all her life.

So, I thank God for Christian parents and grandparents who set a good example for us. Think about it, and in prayer, why don't you thank God too?

I love Mongolia. It is a fascinating place. Maybe I can visit you again next August or September.

Love, Your Colorado Grandpa

CAWS FROM CROW HILL
February 10, 1996

This letter might be called "News from Crow Hill" or What's new from Crow Hill?

You know you can learn a lot from a dog! I learn a lot from Ebony, our *Doberman*. Maybe I should call her a *Doberwoman*. Or maybe she is a *Doberperson*. No, not *Doberperson*. Maybe it is more politically correct to call her a Doberdog.

Anyways, I learn from Ebony. Even though we take the same walks every day, sometimes 3 or 4 times down the same driveway, Ebony considers each walk a "new adventure. She is always excited when we mention "walkies." When we ask "Ebony, want to go walkies?" Ebony goes into a fit, all excited, running around in circles.

When we walk down the old familiar driveway, Ebony goes *sniff, sniff...*, looking for the scent of new deer tracks, new elk tracks, new rabbit tracks, new coyote tracks, new dog tracks. So now I also look for new tracks, sometimes new car tracks.

When I was a kid, I would get bored and my Mother probably got tired of me saying there is nothing to do. But I found that if I built a new puzzle, or built a new fort in the woods, or built a new go-cart, or built a new model airplane or read a new book, then life was exciting like it is for Ebony when we say "walkies."

Even old things have something new that we did not notice before. There might be a piece of gold under that old rock, if we would only look.

The Bible is like that. Job, in his book in the Bible, says that reading the Bible is like searching in a gold mine for new treasure. But if our eyes are closed we don't see anything. So we ask Jesus through the Holy Spirit to open our spiritual eyes and then we see things in old familiar Bible verses that we never saw before. Then we say "Wow!" and "Thank you, Lord!" and life has something new again. I hope you discover something new today.

CAWS FROM CROW HILL
where the deer, and the elk, and the fox, and the coyote, and the rabbits, and the chipmunks, and the squirrels....play.

March 16, 1996

Yesterday morning, I looked out the kitchen window before breakfast and a big red fox with black paws and forelegs ran right up on the rock behind the house. He proceeded to roam around the yard looking for his breakfast.

Spring is coming now and in the mountains this is the time we get the most snow. This brings the elk down in our yard. It also makes things a little sloppy. So you might say this is a bad time of year.

You might say that Good Friday should be Bad Friday too, because that was the day they killed Jesus on the Cross. It looked bad. But that is not right. They did not kill Jesus. The Bible says he went voluntarily to the cross to die in our place for the sins and wrongs we have done—to satisfy God's justice. He could have called 10,000 angels to his rescue, but He did not, because he loved us. That's why we called it <u>Good</u> Friday.

(By the way, did you notice that I capitalize "Bible" and He" in honor of the God's Word and in honor of Jesus?)

That sloppy spring snow--it makes dirty mud, and Grandma does not like Ebony our dog coming in with dirty paws, tracking mud all over the house. But the wet mud makes green grass and helps flowers grow. Likewise, Good Friday led to Easter and the resurrection when Jesus rose from the dead. This means we can live forever!

Little seeds die in the ground and become alive again in Spring. So when we see the new flowers breaking the ground we should think of Jesus and have hope. And when we have hard, dark times, we should thank God that the sun always rises in the morning. You can count on it! Because God is faithful!

(Grandpa sometimes gets carried away, preaching a sermon, because Grandpa is a preacher besides an engineer, besides a professor, besides a Grandpa.)

Look for signs of hope this Spring. Look in nature. Look for Jesus. He is always there waiting for you. (I have tears of joy in my eyes typing that, and I can hardly see the keyboard. Don't ever be ashamed to cry. Keep a soft heart.)

Love, Your Colorado Grandpa

P.S. Homework: Draw a picture that's a sign of spring and a sign of hope.

SIGHTS FROM CROW HILL
(not "Caw" this month, because I haven't seen any crows. More deer than anything.)

April 20, 1996

Sights from Crow Hill:
You know I can see the stars really well from up here in the mountains. In the big city of Denver, the city lights block out the stars. I saw the big comet last month near the North Star. Maybe you could see it in the Upper Peninsula of Michigan. The big comet was called K...., something no one could pronounce.

Forty days after Easter, Jesus ascended (went up) into heaven, and the clouds took Him out of their sight. We call it Ascension Day. The angels said someday we will see him return in the sky.

Did you know that on May 6, 2000 (the day before Harley's birthday) that something will happen in the sky?" The planets Uranus, Neptune, Mars, Venus, and Mercury will all line up with the Earth on the opposite side of the sun in the belt of Orion, a constellation, called the hunter, the glorious one, and the coming one. The three stars in his belt are known as the three kings. Maybe there was a sign there that the wise men saw when Jesus came the first time. Maybe there will be a sign there when He comes again. This line up of five planets plus earth plus the sun occurs only once every 45,000 years.

If the scholars are right, the history of the Bible will be 7000 years old in 2000. There will be 7 planets lighted up. 7 is a sacred number. Maybe Jesus is coming back the day before Harley's birthday in 2000. The Bible says all eyes will see Him. Someday He will take us to heaven with Him. Some do not want Jesus as their Savior, so they will be left behind to suffer.

Maybe 2000. Maybe this year. Jesus says no one knows the day or hour, only God the Father.

Insights from Crow Hill:

What do you see? What are you looking for? Are we looking for Jesus to come someday?

Just like the lights of the city keep us from seeing the stars, other things in life keep us from seeing Jesus. He is everywhere present in the Spirit. We can see Him come alive in the Bible. We can sense Him talking to our spirit or heart if our spiritual eyes are open. We used to sing a song in church. "Open my eyes that I might see, glimpses of truth You have for me."

That's my prayer for me. That's my prayer for you.

Love, Your Colorado Grandpa

CAWS FROM CROW HILL

May 18, 1996

It is dry and hot in Colorado. There is extreme fire danger. Last year was the opposite, very wet. In fact on this day last year we had the worst snowstorm of the year, three days after we brought the Younkers to the airport to leave for Mongolia. Good thing that snowstorm did not come on the 15th. Just goes to show, we can't depend on the weatherman or on the weather, but we can depend on God. In fact the Bible encourages us to depend on God:

Prov.3:5,6, *"Trust in the LORD with all your heart, and do not lean on your own understanding. In all your ways acknowledge Him, and He will direct your paths."*

Yes, it is dry and hot here this year. We need to give the birds and chipmunks and squirrels water every day, or they might die of thirst or move down to the river. We want them to stay here because they are our friends.

Sometimes we get thirsty and dry, and water tastes so good. Sometimes we get thirsty and dry in a different way. We get dry spiritually. The symptoms are we feel bored, down, or discouraged. Maybe we are really thirsty for God. When we have not read the Bible for a while or prayed or thought about God, we might feel like David in the Bible who said, "*As the deer pants for the water brooks, so my soul pants for Thee, oh God,*" Ps. 42:1.

And Jesus said, "*If anyone is thirsty let him come to Me and drink,*" John 7:37. What does Jesus give us to drink? Love, care, assurance, peace, ... Can you think of anything else?

Well they are having a cookout at the Bible camp nearby, and I have to go see if the birds have any water to drink. And I have to bring garbage to the dump, and bring this letter to the post office.

CAWS FROM CROW HILL
June 15, 1996

The last time I wrote, it was dry and hot in Colorado. Two hours after I mailed your letter there was a forest fire 10 miles from here in Buffalo Creek that burned 11,000 acres. Twelve houses and cabins were destroyed and about 1000 fire fighters were brought in from other states to fight the fire. We read in the paper that it is really dry in Mongolia and that 1/5 of their forests have burned. But they have only about 35 fire fighters with only 35 shovels to fight fires over a 2000-mile range.

It reminds me too that the USA has most of the churches and most of the preachers, and the rest of the world has very few. That's why the Younkers are in Mongolia, and why others are in other foreign countries to help them.

Today, Saturday, it is raining and it looks like it will rain all day. Now the people in Buffalo Creek fear flash floods that will wash away the soil and cause mud slides, because the fire burned the vegetation that normally holds the soil in place.

It reminds me that we have many storms and tragedies to face in life. We have to be prepared. If we have our roots down deep (have a deep trust in God), the winds and rain can't move us. And God can keep us from the fires too. Read Psalm 121 where it says God never goes to sleep. He is always watching over us.

I took Ebony for a walk in the rain to get the paper. I had my duck hunting coat on. I have never hunted ducks, but it makes a good rain coat, and it has deep pockets for ducks. But I use it for hunting rabbits, because I can put rabbits in the deep pockets. But today I put the newspaper in a deep pocket to keep it dry in the rain. You know what? God has some very deep pockets, big enough to hold us.

However, my pockets were not big enough for Ebony, so she was soggy wet when we got back, and I had to wipe her dry with a rag. But she was willing to go with me even in the rain. The security of her master holding her leash was enough for her. Who's your Master?

Is it Jesus?

CAWS FROM CROW HILL
July 12, 1996

What's in a name? Why is this mountain called Crow Hill? Well, I thought it was because crows lived here. But I see more birds, chipmunks, deer, and elk than crows. Well, I read in the "Fairplay Flume" (our weekly Park County newspaper) that Crow Hill was named after Harry Crow, the first man to live in the Bailey area. (Mr. Bailey was the second.)

Well, one never knows! I was surprised! Then I wondered why people are called Christians. Is it because some birds called Christians fly around their heads and build nests in their hair? Or is there another reason? Yes, it is because someone, a person lives in their heart and life, a person named Christ. But the other people in the world don't know that. Someone has to tell them. Like I had to find out about Harry Crow from a newspaper writer.

A big coyote, kind of skinny, walked right up our driveway in back of the house one evening while it was still daylight. He was so close we could have shook hands. Then the next morning after breakfast he came back the opposite way and just as close. Maybe he is coming close because he's hungry. People that are hungry or are in need come close also. We need to help them. Maybe we can tell them of someone who can really help them. Maybe we can tell them that Jesus is close, "closer than a brother".

The cross-bill grosbeak birds are back. They come six or eight at a time try to crowd on the birdfeeder and compete with the finches that are always here. The birds are hungry too. Everybody gets hungry. Even our souls, our spirits get hungry. Some people try to satisfy themselves with garbage. Oh, it does not always look like garbage. But the Deceiver, the Devil tries to fool us. So we need to get out the encyclopedia of soul food, the Bible, to check the ingredients, so we can tell the good things from the bad.

Just some rambling thoughts from Crow Hill.

Jesus loves you, and Grandma and Grandpa love you.

CAWS FROM CROW HILL
August 17, 1996

Just like I say, there are not many crows on Crow Hill. In fact, about 20-30 swallows have taken up residence perched on the power lines leading to our house. They don't make any noise but they swoop and dive around catching bugs on the fly for their food.

Something else came out of the sky an hour ago making a lot of noise. It was the emergency helicopter coming to bring someone to the hospital in Denver, 40 miles away. Most birds and animals make some kind of sound. Can you match up the birds and animals on the left with their sounds on the right?

Draw a line to the correct answers.

Crows	Chitty, Chatter
Squirrels	Snort
Humming birds	Caw, Caw
Chicks	Growl
Rabbit	Hissing, clicking
Cat	Peep, Peep
Deer	Crying like a baby
Bird	Meow
Lion	Bark
Dog	Chirp

Need help? When a coyote catches a rabbit at night, the rabbit cries like a baby and wakes us up with a start. Deer have snorted at us during the dark hours. They blow air through their nose to smell better.

Lots of sounds in the air all the time. Many we do not hear unless we have a radio. We hear different stations by tuning our radio to different frequencies of sound. We should listen more than we talk.

That's why God gave us 2 ears and only one mouth. It is important to listen to someone smarter and wiser than us. There is no one wiser than God. I like to listen to Christian radio stations where I can hear God's Word preached or hear Christian music. Sounds from Crow Hill.

Jesus loves you, and Grandma and Grandpa love you.

Your Colorado Grandpa

CAWS FROM CROW HILL
October 7, 1996

Some crows have returned to Crow Hill. Not many—two or three. They are flying around looking for something. The swallows, humming birds, finches, and grosbeaks are gone. They have returned to the south.

Grandpa has returned to Crow Hill after his trip. The chipmunks and squirrels have never left, but they will be hibernating soon, crawling into their holes or nests for the winter. We won't see them again until spring. The doe deer have never left, but the buck deer have been hiding somewhere this summer. They will return soon, however, looking for a girl friend. The elk have returned as the snow has returned to higher elevations in the mountains.

Talking about elk –there were 30 elk hunters from US, Australia, and Germany in line in front of me at the UB airport in Mongolia. They all had big racks of horns they were checking in as baggage. Those elk will never return again.

As you might have guessed, this month's thought or theme is the word "return." The Bible says some evil people return to their evil ways like a dog returns to his vomit or a pig returns to wallowing in the mud. We return to bad habits, or we can return to good habits. If we have bad habits Jesus can help us change and give us power over evil desires. Jesus can help us develop good habits.

What are some bad habits you should not return to? What are some good habits you should return to?

The Bible also says Jesus will return to earth someday. Where will He find us? In Mongolia? In the US? In Michigan ? In good habits or in bad?

If we have left, let us return to prayer, to Bible reading, to love, to worship, and to all the good things God wants for us.

Jesus loves you, and Grandma and Grandpa love you.

Your Colorado Grandpa

CAWS FROM CROW HILL
November 24, 1996

Sorry that this November letter is late. You will hopefully receive it before Christmas.

Grandpa went deer and elk hunting the week of Nov. 2-10, but it was so warm (65 degrees F) and there was no snow, so the deer and elk were hiding up high in the mountains. Also, the hunters from the two earlier seasons had chased them away. But I had fun hiking in new territory. I hiked for miles looking for fresh sign, but to no avail.

A week later after the season was over, it snowed and guess what? Some 20 deer walked through our yard, including 4 bucks. The biggest buck, 5 points per side laid down 20 yards behind our house while the rest of the family fed off our land. It was great watching so many deer until "you know who" spotted them and started barking.

It is almost Thanksgiving time. I was studying Psalm 107 in preparation for our men's huddle (men's group) at our church Tuesday night. I found 6 times where it says in this Psalms that we should give thanks to the LORD. How many times can you find? It says we should give thanks because the LORD is good and that we should thank Him for His lovingkindness. How has He been good to us? How many things can you think of? List them here:

Read Psalm 107 to find reasons for thanking the Lord.

Grandma and Grandpa are traveling to Minneapolis on Thanksgiving Day where on Saturday they will have a 60th wedding anniversary for Great Grandma and Great Grandpa Gerdeen. We will stay at Clint and Martha Younker's house, but they will be gone to their cottage.

Do you have any Thanksgiving time memories? I do. Especially when my Grandma and Grandpa Johnson were living and we always celebrated Thanksgiving together. We can't always be with relatives in this modern age. But we can always be with Jesus – especially if He lives in our heart.

Jesus loves you, and Grandma and Grandpa love you.

Your Colorado Grandpa

Grandpa's Newsletter
January 27, 1997

As you know there will be no more "Caws from Crow Hill." And we asked for help to name a new newsletter. It was so hard to choose from all the suggestions from Mongolia, so Grandpa decided to use several of the names for subheadings, and I came up with the following format (which could change):

Name : ECHOS FROM COLORADO (Mary)

Subheadings: Gunshots from Denver (Pete)
Lakewood Laughs (Joani)
Gramp's Ridge Ramblings (Joani/Lori)
Hairballs From Ebony (Mary)
Hugs From Hoyt (Combination)

Well, let's try it out...

ECHOS FROM COLORADO
Gunshots from Denver: Yes, there were gunshots in Denver. A couple of murders again this last week. The act of murder results when there is hate in our hearts. Let's replace hate with the love of Jesus. The Denver Broncos did not make it to the Super Bowl even though they had the best record. The team closest to Escanaba won. Green Bay!

Lakewood Laughs: Can't think of anything funny. Trying real hard. Oh, Grandma reminded me of something. Two senior citizens and a Doberwoman who were crowded into front seat of pickup piled high like hillbillies were flagged down after seen dragging a kitchen stool down Highway 285 from the mountains. (Who could that be?)

Gramp's Ridge Ramblings: A dozen robins were seen on Hoyt this week. It got up to 58 degrees F today. Is this early spring or what? No, it's typical Colorado weather. We get the most snow in Denver in March. Lots of snow in the mountains now, however, on other side of the Divide.

Hairballs From Ebony: Did you know Ebony likes to eat cat poo? We are glad to move away from the townhouse, because of loose cats and cat poo that Ebony finds. Now why would a well fed dog eat cat poo? Or why would a Christian eat garbage when he/she has the honey of God's Word?

Hugs from Hoyt: Lots of hugs and kisses from Grandma and Grandpa, and licks from Ebony. (I hope it isn't after "you know what?") Grandma will tell you about the new house.

Your Colorado Grandpa

ECHOES FROM COLORADO
February 24, 1997

Gunshots from Denver: The Denver Bronco football team has changed their uniforms and left off the "D". Are they moving to Aurora so they can get a new stadium? Now Denver is offering them the old Stapleton airport site. The negotiations go on. Who will give them the best deal? When you go shopping, who will give you the best deal? Sometimes no choice in Houghton. Lots of choices in Denver.

Lakewood Laughs: Two Texans came to Colorado to go ice fishing on Bear Creek Lake. They had to be rescued. They were all wet and frozen after they cut a hole big enough for their boat. (Just a joke.)

Gramp's Ridge Ramblings: I rambled around our yard and counted 22 trees in our yard. They are evergreens, mostly Colorado blue spruce and aspen. We need to fence in more of the yard for Ebony. We have a nice big deck in back with city views off the ridge. We can see the mountains out the front of the house. We can see the dinosaur ridge too. Maybe we can go tour it when you visit sometime. We can't see heaven from here, but we can see Jesus working in the lives of people.

ECHOES FROM COLORADO
August 9, 1997

Lakewood Laughs:

Sonya and Skye arrived last night on the airplane. Now Skye is the subject of Lakewood Laughs. She sees Sonya reading the newspaper, so Skye has to do the same, but she covers her head with it. She sees Grandpa brushing his teeth so she has to do the same. We are supposed to see what Jesus does and do the same. Jesus sees what the Father does and He does the same. Paul said we should have the same mind as Christ. We are together with you in Mongolia in the same mind and spirit though we cannot be physically present.

Gramp's Ridge Ramblings:

Grandpa, Sonya, Skye, and Ebony rambled around the park this morning. Skye was in a stroller we rented. Ebony was doing her usual things. It is very wet from so much rain so we have to stay out of mud. The sky was hazy so we could not see the mountains clearly. Sometimes we cannot see clearly what God is doing, but we know brighter days are ahead.

ECHOES FROM COLORADO
September 21, 1997

More Ridge Ramblings:

It's the last day of summer and tomorrow is the first day of Fall. The aspens are beautiful gold and orange in the mountains. Not as pretty as the UP, but almost. I remember seeing the tamarack (larch) trees turning yellow in Genghis Khan Park in Mongolia last year. Those trees were huge and I will never forget the fun we had there with the Younkers on a hike up that mountain.

Fall reminds us that things are always changing. But we remember last fall was similar to this fall and we hope to see another because God is faithful and He is in control of our earth, and he is in control of our lives. That helps us sleep well at night. When we wake up He is still there. In fact, He was with us even when we were sleeping, because Psalm 121 says God never goes to sleep because He has to stay awake and protect us. He evidently does not need to sleep.

We had fun with Sonya and Skye too this summer visiting the Black canyon of the Gunnison and sitting in the hot spring water at Mt. Princeton.

When the Younkers were here this summer, we went to the speedway on the 4th of July and saw a racecar with a jet engine that was so loud it hurt our ears. When it took off, the air temperature went up several degrees.

Harley and Grandpa went fishing again at the Redridge Dam near Lake Superior in Houghton. We did not catch as many fish as last year.

We bought 3.3 acres of land at Indian Mountain close to where our former cabin was. Grandpa has started to build a storage shed. Next year he may start on a new cabin. Ebony our dog found a porcupine there. Ouch!

ECHOES FROM COLORADO
November 10, 1997

Sorry I did not write during October. I was too busy, I guess, going to training courses besides teaching myself.

Grandma and I will go to Minneapolis on Thanksgiving Day and then drive to Escanaba to bring Great Grandma and Grandpa Gerdeen to Minneapolis. We will rent a minivan so it will be easier for Great Grandma who fractured a bone in her back and has been in much pain. Great Grandpa can't see to drive anymore. We wish we could visit everybody, but feel we must visit our oldest first before they die and go to heaven.

For Christmas we plan to visit in Grand Rapids where we will see your Great Grandma Burrows who is your oldest. Then we hope to visit our youngest grandchildren Skye on her birthday on New Year's Eve.

So it looks like we won't get up to Houghton to see Tim and his family until later in the spring. Maybe we can spend Christmas with them the following year. Grandpa hopes to go to Mongolia and see you sometime in 1998. Thanksgiving time is soon. What can you thank God for? List a few things here:

_____

_____

_____

For Thanksgiving we usually eat a turkey. Draw a picture below of a turkey.

Did you draw it with feathers or without? I like to eat turkey without feathers.

ECHOES FROM COLORADO
December 7, 1997

"Good" or "great" are some other words that will be used to describe our feelings this time of year when we open our Christmas presents. If we think our gift is better than that of our sister or brother or friend, we might say, "Mine is best."

Questions #1:
Can you think of some other words you might use or you might hear like: *fantastic* or *cool* or *wow* or _____?

Question #2:
Who do you suppose will get the best gift this Christmas? Will it be the child of a millionaire? Maybe the children in the royal family in England? Like Princess Diana's children? Or who?

Question #3:
Do you know what was the greatest gift ever given?

Question #4:
Do you know what word was used to describe the gift?

The Bible in II Cor. 9:15 says, "Thanks be to God for His indescribable gift." God gave us a gift that no word can describe or explain, because it is beyond words. There is no human word known, no English word, no Mongolian word, no *yuper* word, no word at all that we could use for such a great gift.

Question #5:
What is this gift? It is the gift of a Savior born in a manger.

Question #6:
Who is worthy to receive such a gift? The child of a millionaire?

Children in the royal family in England? Like Princess Diana's children? Or who?

The good news is that the poorest of the poor can receive the most expensive gift! Jesus was born in a stable in the straw, not in a king's palace. The mighty God was welcomed by poor shepherds. He came to bring us joy. He came to be our friend. He is God with us. He will never leave us.

You too can receive this greatest of gifts. First, you admit how poor you are without Him. Then just pray, "Lord Jesus, be born in my heart today." And you will be so happy you won't have any words to describe it.

Love, from Jesus
and your Colorado Grandpa

Dear Lori,
Tell the kids that Grandpa grew up with an outhouse and an indoor potty until 1951 when I was 13 years old. We used crumpled pages from the Sears Roebuck catalog. It did not hurt me. I learned a lot reading the catalog.

Love, Dad

ECHOES FROM COLORADO
February 22, 1998

News about Ebony: She is still sick with heart failure and is taking 3 medicines twice a day. She is now on a special expensive diet and is eating some. Grandpa has to get up about once or twice or three times in the night to let her out because one of the medicines makes her urinate more to clear congestion out of her lungs. Grandma lies awake some nights worrying about her. This is probably a small problem compared to those in Mongolia. But pray as we pray for you.

Good News:

We have nice weather: 62 degrees F today. Your Dad said it was in the 40s in Mongolia. Good to hear that spring is coming.

Riddles:

Do you know the definition of an outhouse? It is a good place to start your career as an entre-manure.

Another:

A place to think and stink –the scholar's dilemma!

Question:

Do you know what the horse said which was standing by an outhouse? What in the world is that guy doing in there?

Spiritual:

Christians in this world are in spiritual warfare. We are fighting against evil and the devil. Sometimes a friend says something bad to us and they don't know it. They don't know that maybe the devil had them say it to hurt us. So we have to still love people, and we have to be wise and not let the devil fool us. He is not as great as Jesus. See I John 4:4. When we catch on to the devil's tricks, we can tell him the Colorado expression: Gotcha!

ECHOS FROM COLORADO

April 7, 1998

"Reserved"

This word is in Grandpa's mind this Easter. This is Holy Week on the Church Calendar. It begins on Palm Sunday when we heard a donkey was reserved for Jesus to ride on. No one else had ever ridden this donkey.

When Grandpa went to the hospital he could not park the car anywhere. Some places were reserved for certain doctors.

My parents, your great grandparents in Escanaba, have some gravesites reserved just for them in Gardens of Rest Cemetery.

After Jesus died on the cross there was a tomb (gravesite) reserved just for him. It belonged to a rich man, but it had been reserved for at least 700 years for Jesus, according to Isaiah in 53:9.

The good news is that Jesus has a place reserved for us in heaven if we have a place reserved for Him in our hearts. See John 14:2. I hope that place is a log cabin on a mountain. Maybe it is a room in a castle.

Reserve some time for Jesus this Easter.

MONGOLIAN TRIP REPORT

June 28, 1998

Duration of trip: May 13- May 29, 1998

Key words: **Push, cold, thieves**

Dave Mahler from our church and I went to Mongolia to join the first work team of 9 men from Seattle that was starting to build a 14,000 sq. ft. multi-purpose building in Ulaanbaatar, Mongolia. Our church supported a major part of our travel costs. We left on Wednesday the 13th.

It was the first time I have flown through Seoul, Korea, where we had an overnight stay. Seoul today is a very modern city with many tall buildings, freeways, and their own auto makers. Before leaving Seoul, we were charged for extra baggage weight again. If we could have checked our baggage straight through (if we did not have to stay overnight) we could have avoided this charge: over $100 for Dave and $30 for me.

Upon arrival on Friday the 15th in Ulaanbaatar, we were met by the Younkers. Bill drove another man from Seattle to the workers' apartment, and Lori rented a taxi for us. However, on the way the taxi ran out of gas, and we had to **push** it to a gas station. The grandkids were allowed only to open one suitcase the first night. They had to wait two more days for suitcase 2 and 3 which had gifts and supplies from the US. Dave and I took the minimum of our own work clothes and one pair of work shoes which we wore the whole time.

The next day, Saturday, Bill took all the workers to the largest flea market in Asia. I think it was called the Zah. Anyway, it is place where **thieves** practice full time in gangs with a lot of pushing and shoving. I had my billfold in my front pocket with my hand on it at all times. Another man on our team had a camera stolen, even though he had his hand on it. He did not know until a few minutes later that it was gone. Were we glad to get out of there - it was like a wrestling match! During all this, ave and Bill were separated from the rest of us.

But Dave showed up later with a new leather coat and hat, which he made a good deal on. Bill and Lori have been robbed numerous times. They can't leave their house alone without one of them there or a friend there to watch it. Even though the house is locked, and the fence gate around the property is locked, and they have 3 dogs, **thieves** still break through and steal. Hebrews 10:34 says to rejoice when people steal from you. Can we Americans do that? If we realize the poverty in the world, we are supposed to rejoice when we suffer robbery in the course of serving Him. If you have not read "The Pineapple Story," please do.

Bill and Lori's straw house is not seen as such, since it is plastered inside and out. It really retains the heat. Some homemade solar windows add a lot of passive solar heat. They have an outhouse without a roof and door. It was cold out there some mornings, but one did not need any air freshener nor did we have to run any ventilating fans. Mixed blessings! Think positive!

The first Sunday we went to the new church building they built last fall with straw insulation like the Younker's house. There were about 80 people there including us workers. Dave was fascinated with their hot water heating system which did not work very well last winter. Being a heating and ventilating contractor, he had recommendations to make to improve the system, or better yet, to change it to a hot air system.

The new 14,000 sq. ft building will have an auditorium for a second church, plus rooms for restaurant shops, plus a basement for a Christian school. Bill plans to teach the Mongolians the restaurant business. One restaurant will feature the McYak burger.

Wednesday of the first week, we went with Lori and Bill on a youth retreat at an old Russian military resort. We took the Porgon, the Russian 4-wheel-drive van. It was 24 -30 hours of **pushing** to get the van started when it kept stalling. When it stalled on a hill, we had to push to turn it around. Tough! Besides it was **cold!** Dave, granddaughter Mary, and I slept in a gher. The others had to sleep in a dorm. But we got so **cold** that night it was hard to sleep. The outhouses there had only a hole in the floor and people often had missed the hole at night without lights. But I had my little flashlight with me and was able to maneuver okay. Boy scouts are always prepared.

When we returned the next day to the job site, it was still **cold** and stayed **cold** for the next week and a half with a cold Siberian wind coming from the north. I caught a chest cold the second week but kept working. I hoped I would not get worse, because if you have to go to a Mongolian hospital, they require you to stay a month minimum or send you out to a sanitarium to recover.

I have come to expect a miracle from God in order to survive when visiting Mongolia. This time God healed the electric saw. We had to saw all the rough slab lumber from 2 to 3 feet wide into 2x4's and 2x6's on a table saw. Well, they had burned out the 2-horse motor before we had arrived and had put a 5-horse Russian motor on it. That burned up the pulley. I was asked to bring pulleys from the US, but the table saw was metric so pulleys did not fit. Bill spent a day and found the only metric pulley in Mongolia, a used one which was missing a key. I hammered a key out of a piece of steel rod, which I wedged into the pulley. We sawed a lot of lumber with that saw, 1000's of board feet. The last I knew the saw was still running.

We had to miss church the second Sunday. The only day we could rent a crane to lift up the trusses we had made was Sunday morning. But the crane was a little small, so we had to take down part of the wall to make room for the boom of the crane. I will never forget singing the Promise Keepers' song to myself: "Let the walls come down,"—the walls that we had built.

We had a lot of Mongolian observers who were amazed at how fast and hard Americans work. They could not believe how quick the building was going up.

Bill and Lori were very tired, doing their regular duties as missionaries plus hosting the workers, providing meals, and continually running errands for lumber and supplies. Mary has a good Mongolian friend who slept over a couple of nights. Peter and Joanna helped some on the building. They both have American and Canadian friends who are children of other missionaries.

We were supposed to go on a fishing trip that last Saturday in that Russian van, but refused and decided to stay and work on the building instead, because it would be easier to work on the building than to **push** a van. We also refused another visit to the Zah.

Ulaanbaatar is changing. In 1996 there were twice as many cars than in 1995. Now I saw maybe 5 times as many cars as before. The city is not prepared for the traffic. The streets are bad, partly gravel and big rocks, and partly broken blacktop. Any trip involves many bumps and a few Ow's from Grandpa. Bill drives his Korean small car as fast as he can over bumps, between goats, cows, people and other cars. Mongolians are good at road rage too. Maybe they invented it when they tried to learn to drive.

Another trip to the airport by Bill on Friday the 29th and we were on the long way home.

Pray for the Younkers and other workers in Mongolia. Every day is a struggle, but the LORD is faithful.

I have many pictures to show you.

Home in one piece.

ECHOES FROM COLORADO
October 6, 1998

Gunshots from Denver

It was not a gunshot that killed Ebony but congestive heart failure. She finally died on Thursday Sept. 24. Grandma has been especially sad and has cried a lot. Ebony was Grandma's baby and constant companion, so she misses Ebony very much. It reminds us that we don't have eternal life here on earth, but look forward to living forever in heaven. I will ask God to bring Ebony and TJ back to us in heaven someday. There will be no "hairballs from Ebony" until then.

The Look from Lakewood

Grandpa's teeth hurt. I went to the dentist. My teeth felt good before I went. Grandpa is trying to decide if he should go hunting this weekend. Grandpa will go to Lower Michigan to a meeting in Ann Arbor the first week in November. Grandma may go to Grand Rapids the same time to see Grandma Burrows who fell and broke her wrist.

Wisdom from the Word

The next few weeks I thought I should give you some wisdom from God's Word, the Bible, which has helped me in my life. My 6th grade Sunday School teacher, Mrs. Rinkenberger, made us memorize Psalm 1, and I encourage you to memorize it too. I have never forgotten it.

This month we will memorize the first two verses. Ps 1:1,2 –

"How blessed is the one who does not walk in the counsel of the wicked (ungodly), Nor stand in the path of sinners, nor sit in the seat of scoffers! But his (her) delight is in the law of the LORD, and in His law he (she) meditates day and night."

Whether we are walking, standing, or sitting, which covers a lot, we are not to listen, or follow, or do what is bad for us. In our culture today, they take polls and find out what the majority think, and we are supposed to take our counsel from these results. Young people are tempted to take advice from their peers, other young people, who think you should try drugs, sex, or alcohol.

How many are seeking what God says? Or asking what would Jesus do? Psalm 1:2 says we should be happy and be delighted in reading God's Word and always thinking about Him and His ways. If we do, the promise is that we will be so blessed! That is something like being happy, but more so. It is really having joy from a good conscience.

Now, how do you explain all this simply to someone as young as Skye? Peter, Joanna, Mary and Harley, do you want to try? Grandpa will try. Maybe something like this…People and kids don't know the right way to go; only God does. We will be more happy asking God what to do.

Think about it.

ECHOES FROM COLORADO
November 22, 1998

The Look from Lakewood

We had a windstorm the other night, and the roof of our neighbor's new shed that he was building ended up in our backyard. Also, the wind blew some of his wood straight onto our windows and the new paint job on the north side of our house.

Sows in the South

A man driving his car had to stop for a pig walking up the street in the southern metro area. We sometimes have to stop for dogs and cats, but not for pigs.

Coyotes in the City

Some kids were chased by a pack of coyotes in a park in the suburb of Highlands Ranch. This is the first recorded instance here of coyotes attacking humans. We have had mountain lions attack children before, but not coyotes. This really is the Wild West.

Wisdom from the Word

Remember last month I thought I should give you some wisdom from God's Word that the Bible has helped me in my life. Mrs. Rinkenberger, my 6th grade Sunday School teacher, made us memorize Psalm 1, and I encourage you to memorize it too.

This month we will memorize verses 3 and 4 –"***And he*** *(she)* ***shall be like a tree firmly planted by rivers of water, which yields its fruit in*** *its season, and its leaf does not wither, and in whatever he (she) does he (she) prospers."*

This is the secret to a satisfying, prosperous life. The godly person who loves God and loves to read the Bible shall be like a sturdy, strong tree growing near a river. In Mongolia and in the dry, arid regions of the western US, we don't find trees growing in the desert, but we see trees growing along rivers in the middle of these dry areas. In the dry barren areas we see old, dry tumble weeds being tossed to and fro by the wind.

If you commit your life to God through Jesus Christ, He will plant you firmly along a river where you will grow strong and survive the storms of life.

If not, you will end up confused and tossed about with no source of strength and no direction in life.

The river represents God, the Holy Spirit, who continually satisfies our spirit so we never get thirsty.

If you even want to know where Grandma and Grandpa live or want to know where to find us, you will find us by the River of Life.

I remember a poem we used to recite years ago: "Over the river and through the woods to Grandmother's house we go. The horse knows the way to carry the sleigh through the white and drifted snow." We always went to my Grandma Johnson's house for Thanksgiving and Christmas.

Though we may not be with you in person this Thanksgiving or Christmas, we can still all meet together at the River.

Meet me at the River.

ECHOES FROM COLORADO
January 31, 1999

I am sorry I have not written a letter since November. I have been so busy. I even worked Christmas Eve day and Christmas Day typing a proposal that we had to get in the mail by the end of December.

Then I had to prepare for an interterm course on Rapid Product Development that I taught 8 hours a day for a week. Then I was out of town in Oregon benchmarking schools in Portland and Corvallis.

So, I have been busy! How about you? Busy or bored? When I was your age I would often get bored. My Dad let me build shacks in the woods, or I would make airplane models or something to keep busy.

The Look from Lakewood

We have a new dog, another Doberman. We got her from the Denver dog rescue last Sunday afternoon. Her name is Jade. The precious material called *jade* is a green emerald, but Dobermans are black and brown. We may change her name. Grandma calls her Babe. She is 5 1/2 or 6 years old and bigger than Ebony was. Jade weighs 80 lbs and has long ears. She is not a sissy like Ebony, but Jade wants to be "top dog" and has taken over our back yard and the park. If any other dog comes by, Jade barks and claws the ground and sends grass and tree bark flying into the air. She is very gentle at home, however.

Wisdom from the Word

Remember in previous months, I thought I should give you some wisdom from God's Word the Bible that has helped me in my life. Mrs. Rinkenberger made us memorize Psalm 1, and I encourage you to memorize it too.

This month we will consider the last verses 4-6, where it says the wicked or ungodly are like chaff that the wind drives away, that they will not be able to stand in the Day of Judgment, and that their way will eventually perish.

I noticed when we drove to Kansas City for New Year's weekend to celebrate Skye's birthday that the high winds on the freeway were blowing tumble weeds everywhere. However, the trees were not moved. They were well rooted in the ground.

Psalm 1 tells us that the ungodly will be tossed about like chaff or tumble weeds. This means they will have no direction in life and that they will be confused and uncertain. On the contrary, those who put God first in their life will be secure, stable, and confident.

When the final storm of God's judgment comes, the ungodly will not be standing in God's presence, for the winds have blown them away, but the godly will be standing there.

Who are the ungodly? They are the ones who listen to the big "windbags" promising them the pleasures of sex, money, drugs, etc. They say you don't have to obey your parents. They say you don't have to study. Just have fun.

Who are the godly? They are the ones who say NO to the windbags and listen patiently and quietly for the whisper of God who says in the Bible, "***This is the way; Walk this way.***"

Walk righteously. Be good, be kind. Love God. Love your neighbor. Confess your sin. Receive Jesus. It will be worth it all when the storm comes.

Don't be blown away.

Grandpa's Email
March 2000

Subject: Adult Study for Sunday, Isaiah 53:3-4

Isaiah 53:3, "He was despised and forsaken of men."
He who was called the Son of Man was despised by man.
He who was called the Son of God was rejected by men.
He who was called the Alpha and Omega was forsaken by men.
He whose name was Jesus, Jehovah the Savior, was rejected by men.
And it is still the same today. He is rejected by men.

Matthew 27:30-31 and Luke 18:31-34.
Both Isaiah and Jesus himself said He would be despised. vs 34-- They understood none of these things. Do we understand? Jesus was despised. He had done no wrong. He was tempted in all points like we are, yet without sin. The most cruel and wicked criminal might deserve to be despised and rejected, but not Jesus.

Why? Mark 14:50. Even all his disciples forsook Him and fled. (A certain man "Mark" escapes naked.) If we had been there with Jesus at the time of His betrayal, we would have forsaken and fled too. Do we not value our own necks more than we love Jesus? How often have we heard Jesus betrayed and have forsaken Him, not by fleeing into Samaria, but by fleeing into silence?

On the other hand, might we expect the same. If we follow Jesus, if we would be like Him, will we not be rejected too? Reasons...

(1) *I John 15:18, "**Jesus said, if the world hates you, you know it hated me before it hated you."*** Those who bear the name, have also to bear the shame. Have you been despised and rejected for Jesus' sake? Jesus understands. He was despised and rejected before you were, for your sake.

> *What do we learn?* **The world is no friend of grace.**
> *What do we learn?* **If we represent the true Jesus, we can expect rejection from the world.**

(2) Another reason for rejection is our own sin. Suppose you were a drunkard, drug addict, or degenerate person. You probably would be rejected by some. Have you even felt rejected because of sin or wrong you have done? Jesus understands. He was despised and rejected because of YOUR sin---long before YOU were.

John was a friend of mine. He was manager of Engineering at a company sponsoring my research work. He was someone I had known in a professional way for several years. On a Saturday morning while I was in my study preparing a sermon for Sunday, the phone rang. It was John calling long distance from 500 miles away. He had lost his job. He told me something I didn't know before. He was an alcoholic, but he had hid this fact from me.

One day he comes to the office and is told he is fired and must clean up his office and leave by the next day. He was rejected because of his sin. He said his wife was an alcoholic too. His daughter was on drugs and had left home. I prayed with him over the phone. After that, I wrote him a letter and enclosed a tract on salvation--how to know Jesus as Savior. John and his wife got their lives straightened out, and John got a new job with a competitor.

A year or so later when I was in the area I stopped to visit them. His wife went to Johns' desk and pulled out a letter. She said John saved your letter and reads it often. She said you were the only friend John had. I was John's friend because Jesus was my friend first.

Have you ever felt rejected because of sin or wrong you have done? Jesus understands. He was despised and rejected because of your sin--long before you were.

(3) Even Christ friends can reject us--when the fire gets too hot. Mark 14:50. Even all his disciples forsook Him and fled.

Isaiah 53:3, "A man of sorrows and acquainted with grief and we hid as it were our faces from Him."

Do we see Jesus as Isaiah portrays Him? As one from whom people hide their face? God wants us to see the real Jesus in Isaiah 53. If we do, we will hide our faces from Him. Why will we hide our faces?

(1) Because we cannot stand to look upon such a sorrowful and grief-stricken man. I think of my grandfather on my mother's side. He had been such a strong man. He took me hunting as a boy. But he had a heart attack and a stroke. He was paralyzed over half of his body. This strong man could no longer help himself. I remember him crying like a baby. He was a grief-stricken man, and I could hardly stand to look at him.

What made Jesus hard to look at? He was a grief-stricken man, because our sin made Him so.

(2) Why do people hide their faces? Another reason. Because they do not want to be recognized. The guilty criminal hides his face in the presence of the TV camera. Adam and Eve tried to hide in the Garden. When we see the searching eyes of Jesus in the midst of His sorrow and grief, we hide our faces because the innocent suffers for our sin and shame, we are guilty, not He.

Isa. 53:3 **"He was despised and we esteemed Him not."** John 1:10, 11, He wept in the Garden, no one esteemed Him then. He was scourged, spit upon and beaten. No one esteemed him then. He went to trial alone--surely someone would defend Him--surely someone would object or would cry out--"Do not crucify Him." But no, he had no defense attorney. He was despised and we esteemed Him not.

What do we learn here? We had no part in the great salvation. Man is of no help to Jesus. Jesus suffered alone for our salvation. "He was despised and we esteemed Him not."

I surprised Wanda once when I told her I was in love with Shirley (surely).

Isa 53:4, **"Surely He has borne our griefs and carried our sorrows."**
It was our griefs He bore. It was our sorrows he carried. Isaiah says, "our." He includes his own as well. If Isaiah could see it 700 years before, certainly we can see it 2000 years later.

What do you see? Just a sorrowful man. No, that is not right. Come a little closer and you will see He is carrying you; He is carrying me. (Remember the poem about two sets of footprints, and there was only one set in the sand?)

Ever talk to your soul? Why do you grieve oh my soul? Jesus has borne your griefs.

Surely he has borne them. Surely, you can be certain of this. Why are you sorrowful, oh my soul? Jesus has carried your sorrows. Surely he has carried them. Surely, you can be certain of this.

Note this past tense usage. He has already carried them. It was certain as done 700 years BC when Isaiah wrote this. And Isaiah says, "Surely He has born our griefs (including his) and carried our sorrow (including mine)."

Matthew 11:28-30, "*Come unto me all you that labor and are heavy laden and find rest for your souls. For my yoke is easy and my burden is light.*"

**Yoke up with Jesus and
you will find He carries the whole load.
Praise the Lord.**

Grandpa's Email
Saturday, October 7, 2000

Subject: Loss of Memory

We picked up Dad from the nursing home Sunday morning and took him to church. At noon when we were to take him back to the nursing home to get his clothes, he asked, "What are my clothes doing over there?" He could not remember being here.

I thought maybe loss of memory is a blessing for old people when they forget the many yesterdays when they had to be in a place they never wanted to be.

Then I thought how God purposefully forgets our sins. We pray, "Psalm 25:7, *"Remember not the sins of my youth."* The answer, Psalm 103:12, *"As far as the east is from the west, so far has he removed our transgressions from us."*

Have a good day and mediate on God's forgetfulness and His forgiveness through Jesus Christ our Lord.

Grandpa's Email
Sunday, October 8, 2000

Subject: Loss of Memory Part II

Although Dad (Clarence Gerdeen) had forgotten even being in the nursing home, later after we had taken Dad home, he remembered the nice lady who had helped him get dressed and helped him find the bathroom.

At church that morning, the congregation remembered Mom and Dad, their Christian example, and their many years of service to the church. As the others sang, "Jesus Loves me," Dad sang along. He remembered that song and the others that a group in the nursing home had sung, and he sang along.

Psalm 25:7, *"Do not remember the sins of my youth or my transgressions; according to Your loving kindness remember me, For Your goodness' sake, O LORD."*

God can forget our sins, but still remembers us. How? Because of the Cross. It was on the cross that the thief said, *"Remember me when you come into your kingdom."* And Jesus said, *"Today you will be with Me in paradise."*

**These thoughts will help us remember the Sabbath Day
to keep it holy.**

Grandpa's Email

Sunday, November 19, 2000

Subject: Thanksgiving in spite of tragedy

The Younkers have suffered a tragedy. The pipes in their house in Winner, SD including the "hot" (ice cold) water system have frozen. Damage to floors, carpets, toilets, and hot water tank have occurred.

Our nation's election process is in turmoil, and our future is uncertain.

Here is a perspective from Helmut Thielicke,* a preacher of Stuttgart, Germany during the tragedies of WWII. (The parentheses are mine.)

"But remember this: there is nothing in life--neither fullness nor hunger, neither culture or rubbled ruins, neither home nor far country--that cannot become a vehicle of divine grace when it comes to those who love God. For then it is quite simply a question of taking literally and realistically as possible the promise that "everything works together for good [for] those who love God and are called according to His purpose." The distress we are having to endure now, the worry about what will happen to Germany (or the house in Winner), the anxiety for the future of our deeply confused world, (or our country), the need for food and clothing, and all the other little afflictions are all primarily a question addressed to us. And the question is whether we are going to let all these things lead to sadness, despair, and despondency or whether, for once, we are simply going to

make the tremendous and yet so simple venture of blindly trusting these words of the Lord that they will work together for our good--and that they will do this the very moment we dare to fear these things less than we love God.

In other words, the opposite of fear is not courage (courage is only repressed fear). The opposite of fear is love toward Him who has overcome the world and therefore takes away the fear that prevails in the world. The very troubles the devil stokes up for our despair can also become the material from which the Holy Spirit forms our faith.

Then let us also put our cares and the worries, the anxiety, and the hunger of hearts and bodies in the hand of Him who can change all things, who can turn water into wine, despair into faith, and the fear of the far country into the blessed peace of the children of God"(Thielicke).

Since God will work all things together for good for us who are called according to His purpose for us, let us thank Him in these distressing times, and wait expectantly for the joy and wonder when we see His promise fulfilled.

Note: *Thielicke had great problems with the Nazi regime. When he criticized the Nazi government, he was expelled from a teaching post in 1940. Help came from the Bishop of Wurttemberg who ordained Thielicke and offered him a pastorate in Ravensburg in 1941. A year later, the bishop transferred Thielicke to Stuttgart, where he was a lecturer and a pastor. There he saw many friends injured and killed and found himself without many basic necessities. More than anything else, his preaching during these times was influenced by a closeness to his parishioners with whom he experienced the joys and sorrows of common life.*

Grandpa's Email
June 15, 2001

Subject: *Clarence Gerdeen's Story2Tell*

Clarence speaking at this 50th wedding anniversary service in 1987. He responded to Jim's request for anyone to speak about their memories of Clarence and Barbara. Several people already had, but there was a slight lull in volunteers, so Clarence stood up and spoke:

If nobody wants to talk, I'll talk.

(Laughter from others was heard.)

You want somebody else?

That's okay. You go ahead. You can talk.

You know, I belong to the lay renewal team and we travel over different states. We just came back from Wilmer, Minnesota. In our lay renewal team, we ask people, "If you had three desires in your life, what would they be?" And my desire is—the first one, that I should know the Lord Jesus Christ more truly by reading the Word and through preaching. We know that we are all ministers of the Gospel. We have shepherds that are set aside like Jim, Pastor Magnuson, [Pastor] Odland, but we are ministers of the Gospel. So we have to be in the Word.

And the second wish that I have is that I continue in the Word, that I might be His disciple. That I might know the truth and the truth will make us free.

And the third desire is that all my grandchildren will know my Savior and for everyone that meets me that I will never be ashamed of the Gospel, for it is the power of salvation to everyone that believes.

I have been in the Word now 'pert near' for 30 years, and I remember lots of Scripture and that is something that they cannot take away from you. When you are in the Word, you know the way, the truth, and light, 'cause Jesus said so.

Thank you.

Grandpa's Email

Sunday, September 30, 2001
Subject: Letter

Here is a letter I am sending to the church in Pelkie, MI. Thought you might be interested in reading it too.

Dear Christian Friends at Grace Lutheran Church:

Congratulations on 25 years of faithful service! Your church was founded on the Rock, Christ Jesus. When we have the right foundation, we also have His promise, **"The gates of hell shall not prevail against the church,"** (Matt. 16:18.)

It is with fond memories that I remember the opportunity and joy to teach and preach God's Word in Pelkie. We had good times visiting in your homes and discussing things pertaining to the kingdom of God and the work of the church.

We live in uncertain times. The tragedy of September 11 showed how vulnerable and defenseless the U.S. is and how insecure we are as a nation. This is not the end of the world, but it is the end of the dream world many have depended upon.

It reminds us that the only security is to be in the center of God's will, to be sure of our salvation, and to be sure of our daily repentance and dependence on Him. Nothing can happen to us without coming upon God first for He is our defense and shield.

My ministry started in Calumet, Michigan in 1971 as a Bible study in our house and then in the old Norwegian Church there. I still have a copy of The Lutheran Hymnary and prayer book from that church published in 1913. I read prayers from it every once in awhile. Here is a part of a prayer that I never understood until the 911 call this September: "Be Thou still my fortress as Thou has been my protection throughout the night, for which I thank Thee with my whole heart."

In the past, I really did not feel the need of His protection through the night as I do now. Now when I awake I thank Him for giving another day of grace and another opportunity to serve Him, the King of Kings.

Jesus may be coming very soon, but I pray He will tarry until more of our friends and relatives have come to the knowledge of the truth and are saved.

Sincerely in Christ,

Pastor Jim Gerdeen

Grandpa's Email
Sunday, October 14, 2001
Subject: Men's Retreat

I just got back this afternoon from our Men's retreat. We sang an old song by Keith Green and had teaching on the concept of *brokenness* among other things.

My Eyes are Dry by Keith Green 1978 (Ps. 51:17)

My eyes are dry.
My faith is old
My heart is hard,
My prayers are cold.
And I know how I ought to be
Alive to You and dead to me.

Oh, what can be done
For an old heart like mine?
Soften it up with oil and wine.
The oil is You, Your Spirit of love.
Please wash me anew
In the wine of Your Blood.

Brokenness (Ps. 51:17)

Tragedy, divorce, death of loved ones, sickness, loss of jobs, etc. are sufferings Jesus may be using to break us.

At Holy Communion, Jesus takes the bread (His body), blesses it, breaks it, and gives it to many.

When we are taken hold of by Jesus, He blesses and breaks us, so we can give Jesus to many.

Grandpa's Email
Tuesday, November 15, 2001
Subject: The Voice of God

Last week, one night I was awakened in the wee hours of the morning and all I could think about was the "voice of God." Several Bible verses came to mind. I will share two now and others later.

The first is God's voice in the Garden calling out to Adam, *"Where are you?"* (Gen. 3:9). Of course God knew where Adam and Eve were. But God wanted them to realize where they were—to realize that sin had separated them from Him.

The second is the voice of Jesus, the Son of God saying, **"Come unto me,"** (Matt. 11:28). Even though sin separates us from God the Gospel calls us back to God.

Love from Christ, Jim (Alias Dad, Grandpa, Brother)

Grandpa's Email
Sunday, December 2, 2001
Subject: A Prayer

I am starting to paraphrase some old Norwegian-American prayers. My interest is to examine the theology of their prayers and improve my own prayer life.

Bless me now

-in the Love of the Father

-in the blood of Jesus Christ,

-by the power of the Holy Spirit.

I praise and thank You, O Triune God

-for Your constant protection, counsel and comfort,

-for another night under Your Fatherly care, and

-that in the darkness I had the light of Your grace.

Grant me again that grace

-to empower me to surrender myself to You.

-to You who has given me so many proofs of Your faithfulness.

I need your power to be a steward

-in everything You have given me.

-because it is the right thing to do.

In everything I undertake,

-may You be the beginning and the end,

-may it all honor You,

-may it serve my neighbor in Your love.

Grandpa'a Email
Thursday, October 3, 2002

Subject: Explaining our move

We are planning to move to Springfield, MO by the end of December, the Lord willing. The plan is to retire from the University and become pastor of Immanuel Lutheran Church there. Because you think I am a "crackpot," the attached document on God's call is intended to explain things...We are keeping our cabin in the mountains. For a while we thought we would retire and spend a lot of time in the mountains, for Psalm 121:1 says, *"I will look up to the mountains where comes my help."* But that's not what it says. It says, *"I will lift up my eyes to the mountains, from where shall my help come? My help comes from the LORD* (not the mountains), *Who made* (not only the mountains but all of) *heaven and earth."*

Living in the Midwest, we will be closer to relatives and, hopefully, it will be more convenient to visit with you more often.

Anyway we will be "under the spout where the glory comes out," and you can expect to see a happier Father and Mother, a more blessed Grandma and Grandpa, and more loving friends.

Grandpa's Email
God's Call
October 3, 2002

The Inner Call. It has been a growing burning in my heart and soul the past few years that I should serve the Lord in some type of Christian ministry when I retire from the University. I enjoy nothing more than preaching and teaching the true Word of God and seeing people come to faith in Christ.

The Outer Call. God's plan is to work through His Church and He confirms the inner call with an external call through the Church. A call has come from Immanuel Lutheran Church in Springfield, Missouri and from the Home Mission Board of the AFLC.

The Need. From a survey, Barna found that only 41% of people in the US attend church regularly so that 59% may be considered unchurched. Clegg and Bird state that:

- The unchurched population in the US is the fifth largest mission field after China, former Soviet Union, India, and Brazil.
- It is the largest mission field in the English speaking world.

- Half of the churches in America did not add one new person through conversion in a recent year.
- More churches are closing than are being planted. Charles Arn estimates the ratio as 3 to 1.
- Conversions to other religions and dropouts from Christianity are escalating.
- Church people do not believe much differently than the unchurched.

The Barna survey of church people indicated that only 8% of adults are evangelicals. Only 6% of Lutherans today indicated they are evangelical and only 37% had a Biblical perspective.

In churches that are growing in America today, 80% of the growth is transfer growth, not conversion growth. This is "reshuffling the Christian deck."

There is a remnant among the unchurched that still have a "Christian memory", according to Schaeffer. The problem is that memory fades with each generation so that the need to do something is urgent.

It has been shown that the two main factors leading the unchurched to choose a church are the pastor and his preaching and the doctrines of the church.

The Solution. Our objective must be the pursuit of unchurched people as expressed in the Great Commission of Jesus in Luke 19:10, *"For the Son of Man came to <u>seek</u> and save what was lost."* To <u>seek</u> means we have to pursue the unchurched outside the "four walls" of the church building.

Then we must teach and preach the true Word of God inside the Church building. *"So faith comes from hearing, and hearing by the Word of Christ ,"* (Rom. 10:17.)

The Ultimate Judgments. There is a Great White Throne Judgment coming when those with faith in Christ will join the blessed in Heaven, and those without faith will be sentenced to eternal damnation in Hell.

There is also the Judgment Seat of Christ when we Christians will be judged for our service. What will we have to say to our Lord and Savior Jesus Christ? We will see our worldly works burn up with fire. The only eternal things are the Word of God and eternal souls that will last forever. Will we hear Christ say, "Well done thou good and faithful servant?" May we hear him say, "You shared the Word of God, or you supported those who did." "You showed the love of Christ to the needy ones."

There is Yet Hope. We were all created in God's image and intended to be vessels of honor and mercy. But we became *cracked pots*, contaminated by original sin and broken by our own sins. But if you look closely you will see a warranty label or life-time guarantee on your broken pot. It is the promise of God that says "redeemable". You can trade in your broken vessel for a new one, (John 3:16.)

God's mercy is drawn to the miserable, like a magnet to even rusty iron. God's love flows to the unlovable like a river flows and seeks the lowest level. Jesus said He came to proclaim the Gospel to the poor (in spirit). And I must do the same as His ambassador.

Grandpa's Email
August 2006
Subject: *Kayaking*

I will tell you about two exciting events on our trip to GR and Hart, Michigan. (Wanda will probably write you about other women-related things.) On Monday I went on a ride with Don Wierenga (Wanda's brother-in-law) and his friend Lou on Don's sailboat. I am glad Lou was along to help put up and take down the main sail, because it was a windy day and the waves and white caps were rolling us around. Don lost his hat in the wind. I kept my eyes on the horizon to avoid sea sickness.

On Tuesday am Don Wierenga and I got up early to go on our first kayak ride. We drove 15 miles to the Pere-Marquette River. The owner of the rental place asked if we wanted cushions or life jackets. Don said, "Two cushions."

I said I prefer a life jacket. (Glad I had one.) Sorry I did not have a swim suit and tennis shoes along, but neither did Don.

The owner said "No problem" and drove us 2 miles upriver and said we could just take our time and float and did not have to paddle if we did not want to.

At times we could just drift along and enjoy the scenery. However, we had to paddle hard at times to avoid windfalls and logs in the river. Well, after an hour as I tried to go between two logs, I avoided the first but the current took me broadside into the biggest log and rolled me over upside down. (that's where I must have lost my hat.) I managed to right myself grab the kayak and paddle and hang onto the log and catch my breath. The next few minutes I managed to fight the current and follow the log to shore, dragging the kayak and paddle in about 4 feet of water. I came to a steep bank about two feet above the water, but with the kayak full of water, it took me a while to tug and pull to finally get the thing up on the bank, to turn it over and get most of the water out. Don was downstream waiting and treading water. I hiked down a few yards to find a more shallow place to launch out again. Then went back and dragged that kayak to the place.

We finally made it to our destination with me soggy wet from head to toe, including my billfold, car keys, and sunglasses that had managed to stay on.

Back at the house in Hart, I hung all my wet clothes including my wet shoes and wet underwear, socks, pants, and shirt over the front porch railing to dry. After a comment that "it looked like a redneck from Missouri had moved in," I moved all the wet stuff to the back railing. I laid my 20 dollar bills and wet billfold in the bedroom window to dry in the sun.

I praise the Lord I did not hit my head on that log or lose the keys to the rental car or lose my billfold.

Lessons learned:

1. Kayaking can be fun to a point.
2. Do not go kayaking without a life jacket no matter what anyone says.
3. Wear a swim suit and lock the rest of your clothes and valuables in your car, and secure your car keys to your body or swim suit with a chain and a hook somehow.
4. Kayaks roll over easily.
5. Do not let your kayak get broad side to the current if you can help it. Or better yet, don't go kayaking in the first place. If you do, be sure you know the Lord and have no unsettled accounts with Him.

Finally, maybe you should listen to your mother-in-law if she says not to go on any adventures with your brother-in-law.

Meanwhile back at home, I have been asked to teach an online course again at Missouri State University and have started preparing for it. It is IDM 610 "Project Leadership."

Kayaking is not one of the topics!

Grandpa's Email
Tuesday, July 31, 2007
Subject: Reflections on my parents' legacy

As you know Father and Mother's house and land was sold, and closing occurred on Friday, July 27, 2007. The sale went quickly within two months after opening bids. The sale price was higher than expected. There were no conditions on the sale. No repairs to be made by us. This quick sale happened at a time when the housing market was down.

I believe this was the Lord's doing. Reflecting in this, I believe we are still being blessed by our parents' devotion to God. God promises those who live by His Word "*that it may go well with you and your children after you...*" (Duet. 4:40.) This promise is repeated 10 times in the book of Deuteronomy.

A tithe to the Lord on our inheritance may be a way to show gratitude.

May we also pass this blessing on to our children.
Blessed be the Name of the Lord.

Conversational English: A Bridge to the Gospel
Shared with the professors at Faculty Commons,

November 13, 2009

At the International Community Church on the University of Missouri campus, we provide a free Conversational English Language program for international scholars to practice and increase their English language skills in an educational format. I am one of three volunteer teachers. On Tuesdays I teach engineering, scientific and professional English vocabulary in the context of readings and presentations which we then discuss. The scholars are a mix of Ph. D. students, post docs, short term visiting international researchers or their spouses. The scholars are 40% Chinese, 40% Korean, and 10% other nationalities.

At mid-semester I started an optional Bible English class for a second hour. (By this time we have developed a rapport with each other.) We do a word study from the first chapter of the Gospel of John. This semester the words for the last four weeks were: Word (logos), beginning (genesis), light and darkness, and receive and believe (have faith). (I also cite how these words are also used in everyday English. For example, *genesis* relates to origins and genetics and DNA.) At the conclusion of each study, I testify what this means to me. For example, I said, " Jesus is the Word, the logos, reason or essence of meaning. What this means to me is God has the last word. God had the first word. His word is absolutely true. I can stake my life on it."

This last Tuesday, a "God thing" happened. Seven had stayed for Bible English as we discussed what it means to receive and believe (have faith). They started asking questions like "How can I prove that God exists?" "What about evolution?" "What do you mean by eternal life?" This was a little departure from our text, but I went on to say we have three clues (evidence) of God's existence: the witnesses, prophets and apostles who testified in the Bible, the internal witness of our conscience, and the evidence of creation (we then read part of Romans 1 together). One lady, who had told me she a year ago that she had never heard anything like this about God before , now said, "I believe in God." We went on to discuss natural evolution, theistic evolution, micro and macro evolution, intelligent design, and creation. But I said that is not where I start. "I start with Jesus. He claims to be the Truth." I shared the gospel and we then read John 14:6 together. The main question is do we receive Him and believe (have faith)?

Then we had to leave. We will continue next week. But before we left, three of our scholars were anxious to have a free copy of the three Gospels of John I had left. I have given away ten this past year and this week I ordered ten more. Afterward one lady asked what does the word Gospel mean.

It is certainly a blessing to see God working! May many of these scholars come to true faith in Him.

Grandpa's Email
March 2011
Subject: End Times

The tragedy in Japan reminds me of research I have been involved with. From 1965 and for more than 20 years I was involved with the Pressure Vessel Research Committee in NY. Much of our work involved analysis of the containment vessels for nuclear reactors. They are the safest structures ever designed. (Also I was a consultant in 1989-90 for a vessel being designed in Switzerland.)

There are many confusing reports from the media about the mechanical equipment. The problem is not the design. The tragedy in Japan is a natural catastrophe, earthquake and tsunamis of enormous proportions.

The small nuclear radiation leaks from steam so far are 100 times less than you get from a CAT scan. The containment vessels so far have prevented radiation to the surrounding area except for workers in the plant trying to cool the reactor core.

This tragedy and others should cause the world to think of the fact that this world will not last forever. The Bible prophecies in Matt 24 and Revelation 8 tell of worse tragedies to come when one third of the world [will be] destroyed by fire, a third of the sea and a third of the rivers being affected. This happens even before the judgment of God in Revelation 16. God is allowing these tragedies hoping people will repent. Pray that many will.

Matthew 24:8

*"But all these things are merely
the beginning of birth pangs."*

Matthew 24:14

*"And this Gospel shall be preached
in the whole world for a witness in all the nations,
and then the end shall come."*

Let's be about the Master's business.

Finding Purpose in Life in Retirement, My Story
by James Gerdeen

My life has been one with two careers but with one overall purpose. While being a Professor of Engineering and a Pastor of churches at the same time, the challenge has been to glorify God in all that I do, (I Cor. 10:31.) It has been 12 years now since retirement from the full-time faculty position in Colorado and the move to Missouri. The places and situations have changed but the purpose remains the same. As Pastor Sidney Swensen of St. Paul used to say "I am not retired but refired !" I am still doing some of the same things but at a slower pace.

Living with a purpose in the will of God brings peace and joy. Let me share some advice from the Scriptures that have guided me and hopefully will help you who are in a similar stage of life. It is assumed that you have a personal living faith in the Lord Jesus Christ.

First of all, we should learn that *being* a Christian is more important than *doing* Christian work. Peter emphasizes that we make every effort to be sure that certain virtues are evident and growing in our lives, namely these: diligence, faith, moral excellence, knowledge, self-control, perseverance, godliness, brotherly kindness, friendship, and agape love. He goes on to say these virtues will keep us from being ineffective and unfruitful, (II Peter 1:5-8.) I began to realize this when a former student (1977) gave me a gift of a slab of lode copper with this verse inscribed that he said reminded him of me: *"I delight to do Your will, O my God; Your Law is within my* heart," *(Psalm 40:8)*. I always remember what my Mother underlined in my Bible and challenged me with when I left home for college in 1955, *"but grow in the grace and knowledge of our Lord and Savior Jesus Christ"* (II Peter 3:18). And before that in 1952, my confirmation pastor, Pastor Ringstad had challenged me with Matthew 6:33, *"But seek first His kingdom and His righteousness, and all these things will be added to you."*

A commitment to these Scriptures was made early in my adult life and by God's grace will continue. So far these principles can apply to any Christ follower. But who am I (are you)? How do I (you) fulfill God's particular calling in this stage of my (your) life? How has God prepared me (you) for the next step? Personally, I am a professor and a pastor. I am a father, grandfather, and husband. Some relationships are the same, but there are some new applications now as life has changed during retirement. The applications are to fulfill my current vision of what God calls me to do. This includes:

- **To reserve time** for prayer, worship, Bible study, exercise, hobbies, and rest to keep body, mind and spirit refreshed.

- **To seek to have a Christian influence** with faculty on the University of Missouri campus. This includes weekly Bible studies and discussions.

- **To focus my efforts** on the international scholars here. God has given me the desire to see them come to know our Lord and Savior Jesus Christ. To build bridges by hosting free conversational English classes and offering academic advice to graduate students.
- **To continue to preach** on a part time basis and to be on call to fill in at the International church here in Columbia, Christ Lutheran in Stover, and New Hope Lutheran in Laurie, MO.

- To continue to love my wife as Christ loved the Church.

- To continue to love and support our children and grandchildren as God our heavenly Father loves and supports us.

God calls each of us in different ways. How has God prepared you for this time in your life? Carpenters and handy men help build churches. Many go on short term mission trips. Others prayerfully and financially support those who go. We have a 91 year old lady here who takes delight in baking cookies for our internationals and shares them during the time for refreshments.

The book, *The Call* by Os Guinness has helped to keep God's call fresh in my mind during these recent years. There are 25 chapters and at the end of each chapter he adds: *"Listen to Jesus of Nazareth; answer His call."*

Some of us may think of retirement as only relaxation on the beach. However, think of how God called and used Abraham, Moses, Caleb and others in their old age. If you are feeling restless maybe God is calling you. On a family trip, the restless child asks his father, "Are we home yet?' God is our heavenly Father. Some of us, His children, are not home yet. There are people yet to reach and places for us to serve.

EPILOGUE

Dear Peter, Joanna, Mary, Harlan, Skye and Connor,

My brother Joel and I have been doing a genealogy search, and I wish my Grandparents had told me more about their families. It would have made our searching easier. So I will tell you a little and you may ask for more if you wish. You may also ask your parents to read a copy of our report of our trip to Sweden and Norway for more particulars.

On my Father's side, his mother, my Grandma Anna Sophie Gerdeen, died when I was only 2 years old and I don't remember much. She had five children, three boys and two girls. She had diabetes that evidently contributed to her early death.

My Grandma Anna Johnson, on my mother's side lived near us, and I was fortunate to have spent much time with her from my birth through my early years up through the time I left home for college. She had much influence on me especially because she was a godly Christian. She said I would be a pastor someday. I did not believe that at the time, but evidently she had been praying that I would. She also told me not to smoke because if God wanted me to He would have put a smokestack on top of my head. She also told me to be sure I married a Christian girl. As a result I was careful not to date during my high school days.

I met Wanda, your Grandma at a summer job at Gardner Denver in Grand Haven, Michigan. That was the summer of 1958. I found out she was a devout Christian and started dating her. In the Fall I had to go back to college at Michigan Tech 500 miles away. We wrote love letters to each other each week. I referred to her as "my wonderful Wanda." I think Wanda still has all my letters. I drove to Grand Haven in my '51 Chev to see her whenever we had a holiday break, even once through a blinding snowstorm. We were engaged in March 1959, I wanted to get married soon like that coming summer, but Wanda made me wait until August 1960, a year after I started work as an engineer in Columbus, Ohio. Then I was driving once a month on weekends 350 miles to see her.

I had a secret—I was smoking cigarettes. (Remember what my grandma had told me?) I knew Wanda would not marry me if she knew. I had to ask the Holy Spirit to help me quit. He did.

Wanda, your grandma, was very faithful in supporting me. She typed my Master's thesis. She gave up an office career to be a wife and mother, a "domestic engineer" and "domestic artist" she would say. She was with me in many moves as we lived in many different places. She made up for my absence in the home when I had two jobs as both a pastor and professor. Like her mother Grandma Burrows, she believed "Cleanliness is next to godliness." I had the cleanest clothes and the cleanest home in town. Any success in my life would not have been possible without her.

Proverbs 31:30
"Charm is deceptive, and beauty is fleeting;
but a woman who fears the L*ORD* *is to be praised.*
31 Honor her for all that her hands have done,
and let her works bring her praise at the city gate."

--**James C. Gerdeen**, *October 2015*

APPENDICES

Appendix A: Jim, the Engineer

In 2011, James Gerdeen was honored as an outstanding graduate of Michigan Tech University and inducted into the ME-EM Academy as one of their most successful individuals from the 11,000 alumni. These inductees are chosen as role models for future students. His photo hangs in the halls at MTU. Here is the description given about my father on page 32 of the ME-EM 2011 Annual Report.

Dr. James Gerdeen (BSME '59) retired as Professor and department of Mechanical Engineering Chair from the University of Colorado-Denver. After graduation, Jim worked in industry before completing his MS in 1962 from Ohio State University and later his PhD from Stanford in 1965, both in mechanical engineering.

He returned to Michigan Tech as a faculty member from 1968 to 1989. He received his Master of Divinity, Theology, from the Free Lutheran Seminary, Medicine Lake, Minnesota, in 1980 and has served various churches as lay pastor. Jim continues to teach online courses in Industrial Management at Missouri State University and technical English classes at the University of Missouri.

Internationally recognized for his research and expertise in pressure vessel design, structural analysis, metal working manufacturing, and mechanical design, Dr. Gerdeen is the author of or co-author of sixty-five plus papers and 100 plus research reports.

His honors and awards include the Michigan Technological University faculty Research Award (1974). Society of Manufacturing Engineers Educator of the Year-Western Region (1998), University of Colorado Faculty Service Award (2001), and a Decade of Excellence Award from the University of Colorado Denver (2003).

Jim served as a treasurer of the Michigan Tech Alumni Association Board of Directors from 1970-1974. He and his wife, Wanda, have three children: Lori, Sonya, and Timothy. The Gerdeens reside in Columbia, Missouri.

Appendix B: The Colorado Years

James Gerdeen
Department Chair / Professor
Mechanical Engineering Department
University of Colorado at Denver
1200 Larimer St.
North Classroom Building, Room 3502
Denver, CO 80217

Courses Taught:

Solid Modeling Using Pro/E

Finite Element Analysis Using Pro/Mechanica

Methods of Engineering Analysis

Properties of Engineering Materials Lab

Rapid Product Development

Manufacturing Seminar

Theory of Elasticity

Research Interests:

sheet metal forming (automotive and beverage cans)

polymers and composites

pressure vessels

rapid prototyping

electronic manufacturing

electronic packaging

stress analysis of printed circuit boards

plasticity

creep

fatigue

fracture mechanics

Consulting:

Battelle, Alcoa, Chrysler, Ford, General Motors, US Bureau of Mines, USAF, NASA, Motor Wheel Corp, Whirlpool, Ball Packaging , Pillsbury, Lear Ziegler, Gardner Denver, Pre-Finish Metals, Abbott Labs, Michigan Gas Co., Proctor & Gamble, Coors, Gates, Budd Co., US Ind. Chemicals, PVRC/WRC, NSF, Argonne Labs, Sandusky Foundry, Libby Owens Ford, Latrobe Steel, HITCO, AISI., Animal Care, NREL